Living with Autism

BY JEFFREY POWELL

The Successful Steps to Recognizing, Adapting, Learning, and Understanding Autism

2nd Edition

Table of Contents

Introduction..4

Chapter 1: What is Autism?................................5

Chapter 2: Presentations of Autism 9

Chapter 3: Diagnosis of Autism..........................13

Chapter 4: There is Hope for your Child............20

Chapter 5: Autism Treatment 24

Chapter 6: Autism Management 29

Chapter 7: Autism Awareness............................46

Chapter 8: How You Can Help Your Child.........51

Conclusion 60

Check Out My Other Books 61

Introduction

I want to thank you and congratulate you for purchasing the book, *"Living with Autism: The Successful Steps to Recognizing, Adapting, Learning, and Understanding Autism"*.

This book contains proven steps and strategies on how to help your child or loved one cope with autism. Receiving the news that your child has autism can be very terrifying and you may succumb to feelings of depression and being discouraged. Through this book, I hope that you will understand that there are a lot of things that you, as a parent, can do to help your autistic child to live a meaningful life. You just need to fully accept your child for who he or she is and take delight in the beautiful things that your child brings into your life. I hope that through this book, you will find the inspiration to successfully deal with your child's autism.

Thanks again for purchasing this book, I hope you enjoy it!

Chapter 1: What is Autism?

Autism is characterized by serious and insidious impairments in a number of vital areas of development that include reciprocal social interactions and communication, behaviors and imagination. A person can only receive a diagnosis of autism if these behavioral symptoms are already evident by the age of three. Even though some parents observe that there is something wrong with their babies, it is quite hard to make a diagnosis of autism before the baby has reached the age of 18 months. The reason for this is that the behavioral symptoms that are required to be established for a person to be diagnosed with autism are not normally apparent until after 18 months.

Most children who have been diagnosed with autism also suffer from some form of learning disability or mental handicap but there are several of them who are known to have average intelligence. Many autistic children also experience epilepsy, visual impairment and hearing disability which are usually overly represented in this particular group of children. People diagnosed with Asperger's syndrome which is a condition that resembles autism normally have average or above-average intelligence.

A rough estimation reveals that one to two children for every one thousand have autism and it has been noted that more boys have autism as compared to girls.

Causes of Autism

Autism is basically a condition that is behaviorally defined but it has several different causes which are both known and unknown. The causes are mostly biologically-based dysfunctions in the brain that impact the ability of the brain to process information. Autism is considered a neuro-developmental ailment and it was noted that most cases have a genetic factor in them. The different ways that we process information like how we perceive, process and interpret information, how we learn new things and how we behave in a well-adapted way all lead to the behavioral deviations that are observed in autistic people.

Scans of the brain reveal dissimilarities in the shapes and structures of the brains of autistic children as compared to the brains of children who are considered to have typical neurological development. Several research studies have been conducted to investigate several theories that include the connections of heredity and underlying medication condition to autism.

In a number of families, it is apparent that there is an autism pattern within the family which basically supports the theory that autism has a genetic factor. But the research studies do not show that there is specific gene that is determined to be causing autism. But the researches are continuing their search for abnormal sections of genetic code that the children with autism might have inherited from their parents. It is also evident that there are indeed some children who are born with a vulnerability to autism but the actual "trigger" that results to the development of autism has not yet been identified.

Other research studies investigate the likelihood that under specific conditions, a group of unstable genetics might impede with the development of the brain which then results in autism. But there are other research studies that investigate the problems that occur during pregnancy or the delivery of the baby as possible causes of autism. Still other research studies look at how certain environmental causes like viral infection, metabolic imbalance and contact with environment chemicals may also cause autism.

Genetic Susceptibility

It has been noted that autism is likely to occur more often than expected amongst people who have particular medical conditions like the Fragile-X syndrome, tuberous sclerosis, inborn rubella syndrome and phenylketonuria or PKU that remains untreated. There are also specific dangerous substances that are ingested while a mother is pregnant that are linked with the increased risks of autism.

Environment Factors

Research studies also show that there are other factors other than genetics that contribute the continuous increase in autism cases. One of the most common factor are the environmental toxins like heavy metals like mercury which are now more rampant in our environment compared to prior years. It has been shown that people with autism or those who have higher risk factors are particularly susceptible to these environmental factors because their metabolism and detoxification abilities are compromised by autism.

Chapter 2: Presentations of Autism

Social Interaction

The most prominent facet of autism is often the struggle with reciprocal interaction with other people. This can be pretty apparent even at a very early age when babies might struggle when they use and understand eye contact, facial expressions, gesture and voice intonation while they interact with other people. A lot of children with autism are not able to demonstrate social or emotional reciprocity and they cannot instinctively and spontaneously communicate their enjoyment with their mom and dad nor seek them out when they want comfort. Children with autism are also not always concerned with other children who are of the same age. And even if they can get themselves involved with other children, they normally struggle when they make and keep friends.

Communication

Persons with autism normally experience delay in developing their language skills or complete lack of development at all. Unlike the deaf or the mute who compensate for their inability to speak or hear, persons with autism do not use nonverbal communication to compensate for their undeveloped language skills. Around 50 percent of children with autism were reported to have never developed their speech. And the children who do develop their speech show a vast disparity in skills. There are children who are only able to use single words. While other children may be able to use a lot of words and use them correctly, many of them merely repeat stock statements or phrases that other people have said not considering the situation. There are a small percentage of children with autism who have communication skills that are well developed and can spontaneously speak their language.

Generally, all people with autism struggle in starting and keeping conversations and all of them have inadequacies in understanding language. It is also noted that they are particularly impaired when it comes to understanding the deeper meanings of a language. Even those who are able to expand their vocabulary and communicate spontaneously, it is quite normal for them to have inflexible and literal interpretations of language.

Behavior

It is also common for children with autism to become absorbed in a limited range of behavior, interest and activities in a recurring and stereotypical manner. For instance, a child with autism may focus intensely on a particular activity like spinning the wheels of a toy truck or stacking blocks over and over again. It is very seldom for them to be involved in spontaneous and changeable games like pretend and role playing. It is also common to observe them being fixated on various objects and on highly complex habits and patterns that should be repeated in precisely the same manner every time. When they are not able to do the habit or routine in exactly the same manner, it may result to an explosion of despair or anger. Any kind of change like being in a different location or doing a familiar activity in a different sequence than normal can also be quite difficult to bear for people with autism. Some children with autism who are somewhat older and are more well-endowed may particularly have phases of one-side and focused interests like memorizing time table, other people's dates of birth and other facts and data. Other common behaviors of children with autism include the continuous waving of their hands, rocking back and forth and walking on tiptoe.

Other than the behaviors mentioned in the first chapter that are used in diagnosing autism, other signs and indications that are commonly seen in people with autism include being overly sensitive or under sensitive to a particular sound, touch or odor, hyperactivity which comes in phases and problems with sleeping and eating. But these behaviors are not really required to be present for a person to be diagnosed with autism.

Considerable Variations

It is normal for people with autism to be considerably different from one another in several ways even though the effects of having autism are always severe. For instance, the extent of autism is known to differ from serious to mild. Likewise, their level of skills and abilities can differ from serious learning disabilities to having above-average intelligence. It is quite common for people with autism to have other health conditions like different genetic syndromes, epilepsy, depression, anxiety or attention deficit and hyperactivity disorder. A person may therefore suffer from severe autism as a part of multiple impairments that may include moderate to serious learning disability and epilepsy. If that is the case, the person with autism may have maximum disability. On the other hand, it is possible for a person to have a lower degree of autism and high degree of skills and abilities. The dissimilarities in the level of gravity of the behavioral expression of autism is quite huge and also depends on the person's own personality, age and degree of development.

Chapter 3: Diagnosis of Autism

In the previous chapter, we talked about the different presentations of autism and learned that these presentations vary from one afflicted person to the next. There are numerous symptoms and they may even appear on normal children. So, what does it take to diagnose autism?

Quick Aside: About Mechanism

Let's talk a little about the condition's mechanism. As of today, how autism occurs is not yet fully understood. There are two areas of its mechanism: pathophysiology and neuropsychology. These are technical terms but fortunately, there's no need to worry about them for this book's purposes. So, why mention them?

Well, that would be for the discussion on diagnosis. The mechanism, as well as the causes, of autism is not yet understood well. Because of that, the diagnosis of autism is based on behavior.

Diagnostic Criteria and Methods

To conclude with a positive diagnosis for autism, the following criteria must be met:

- At least a total of six (6) symptoms must be present, including:
    - At least two (2) symptoms under the category of qualitative impairment in social interaction;

- o At least one (1) from qualitative impairment in communication; and
- o At least one (1) symptom of repetitive and restrictive behavior.
- Onset must be before the child is of age three.
- The observed disturbances must not be better attributed to childhood disintegrative disorder or Rett syndrome.

There are many instruments used in autism diagnosis. When you go to a pediatrician or any health professional for diagnosis, it may involve you or the concerned child. The two most common instruments are:

• The Autism Diagnostic Interview – Revised (or ADI-R). This is a semi-structured interview for the parent.

• The Autism Diagnostic Observation Schedule (or ADOS). This one, on the other hand, uses interaction with an observation of the child.

Another notable instrument is the Childhood Autism Rating Scale (or CARS). This is used extensively under clinical environments. The objective is to gauge the severity of the condition by observing the children.

Usually, a pediatrician will conduct a preliminary investigation. He/she will take developmental history and conduct a physical examination of the child. This is to evaluate whether further diagnosis is necessary.

If the preliminary investigation warrants further evaluations and diagnosis, they will be conducted. The pediatrician works with specialists in the study of autism. They will observe and assess the child based on several factors including, but not limited to, communication, cognitive, and family. They will also take into consideration any related medical conditions. Oftentimes, a pediatric neuropsychologist will be asked to perform a cognitive skills and behavior assessment.

There are several conditions that may present similar symptoms. So, professionals also conduct differential diagnosis considering hearing impairment, specific language impairment and intellectual disability. Autism can cause difficulties in diagnosing psychiatric disorders that may already be coexisting with it – for example, depression.

If a diagnosis of autism is made, clinical genetics tests are usually conducted especially if other symptoms are suggestive of a genetic cause. These tests may include fragile X testing and high-resolution chromosome testing. These are actually the only two included in the consensus guidelines in both USA and UK. However, many other testing methods have adequate accuracy.

Sometimes, autism is diagnosed at 14 months of age. The stability of diagnosis continuously increases throughout the first three years of a child's life. As an example, it would be less likely for a one-year old child who meets the autism diagnostic criteria to do so a few years later than a three-year old child. The recommendation from the UK's National Autism Plan for Children is a maximum of 30 weeks starting from the first suspicion to the finalized diagnosis. However, few cases have been handled on such short duration in actual practice.

Autism symptoms may begin in early childhood, but it is not impossible to miss them. There are cases when adults request diagnoses for help in understanding themselves or gain understanding from friends and relatives. The objectives of some are related to work as employers might need to make adjustments. In some places, a diagnosis of autism will enable the person to claim benefits, like living allowances for disability.

Over-diagnosis and under-diagnosis may happen, but are rare as of now. Some providers of treatment options may over-diagnose children with unclear symptoms because there is incentive for them. On the other hand, the costs and difficulty in obtaining payment are causes of under-diagnosis. Impairment in vision also inhibits diagnosis. This is because the diagnostic criteria include some that depend on vision. Also, autism shares some symptoms with common blindness syndromes (blindisms).

Classification

Autism belongs to the classification Pervasive Developmental Disorder (or PDD). There are five conditions under the classification – characterized by extensive abnormalities of communication and social interactions, severe restriction of interests, and high level of repetitive behavior. Such symptoms do not indicate fragility, sickness, and/or emotional disturbance.

Within PDD, closest to autism is the Asperger syndrome in terms of signs and probable causes. Childhood disintegrative disorder and Rett syndrome have some common symptoms with autism, but probably have unrelated causes. If the symptoms do not meet any criteria for a specific disorder, a diagnosis of PDD-NOS (stands for "PDD not otherwise specified") is made – this is also called atypical autism.

Autism is commonly grouped together with Asperger syndrome and PDD-NOS – collectively called autism spectrum disorder (or ASD). Thus, autism terminology can get confusing. In this book, we are using the term autism in reference to the classic autism disorder. However, clinical practitioners use ASD, PDD, and autism interchangeably.

Autism manifests across a wide spectrum – from mild to severe. Some individuals may be high functioning, just with verbose pedantic communication, interests that are narrowly focused, and peculiar social approaches. Some individuals show extreme impairments like silence, developmental disability, and repetitive behavior such as rocking and hand flapping. The rest are in between. This behavior spectrum is continuous.

As a result, the boundaries of diagnostic categories are arbitrary at best. Some base classification on IQ levels – dividing the syndrome into low-functioning autism (LFA), medium-functioning autism (MFA), and high-functioning autism (HFA). Some base it on how much aid the individual needs form day to day. You should be aware that these classifications are not standardized. In fact, they are controversial.

Screening

More or less 50% of parents who have children with autism (or any of its ASD brethren) notice unusual behavior/s in the child by age 18 months. Around 80% do so by 24 months. There are several milestones listed in one article published in the Journal of Autism and Developmental Disorders. According to that article, those milestones when not met are definite indications of a need for further evaluations. If this is delayed, it will hinder early diagnosis and lower the chances of success of treatments. The milestones are as follows:

- Absence of babbling by age 12 months.

- Absence of gesturing by age 12 months.

- Absence of single words by age 16 months.

- Absence of spontaneous two-word phrases by age 24 months.

- A loss of any social or language skills, regardless of age.

In the US and Japan, they screen all children for ASD at two points – age 18 months and 24 months. They use tests for formal screening specific to autism. In the UK, only children who show possible signs of autism are screened. As of now, it is not determined which of these approaches is more effective.

Your Part...

As a parent/guardian of the child, you must do your part in order to help with the accuracy of the diagnosis. You won't need to study the conduction of the tests – leave those to the experts.

Your part is in cooperation. You must listen well to the pediatrician or health professional during the tests.

Answer the diagnostic questions as detailed as you can. Encourage other family members to do so as well if they are involved in the history interviews.

You should also support your child in the diagnostic process. The child will likely have difficulties with cooperating because of the condition. While the health professionals will know what to do, you can ease things up by offering full support to your child.

Don't Wait

Diagnosis is just for confirmation. There is no harm in starting treatments before you receive a formal diagnosis. This will be discussed further in a later chapter.

Chapter 4: There is Hope for Your Child

If you have a child with autism, there are several things that you can do to help your child overcome his or her challenges. But it is vital that you ensure that you are also getting the support that you require. When you are looking after your child who has autism, do not look at the act of taking care of yourself as being selfish because it definitely is a necessity. When you are able to strengthen yourself emotionally, you will be able to become the best parent to your child who needs you. The tips that you will read in this chapter aim to aid you in making the life of your autistic child a lot easier.

If you have just learned that your child has autism, you most probably wonder and worry about what will happen to your child. It is always very difficult for parents to learn that their children are anything but happy and healthy kids. Receiving a confirmed diagnosis that your child has autism can really be terrifying. You may like you are not sure what the best help your child should get or you may become confused with the different and sometimes conflicting treatment recommendations that you get. You may been heard some people tell you that there is no cure for autism and that it is a lifetime disorder. These things can really leave you anxious that there is nothing you can do that can make a difference in your child's life.

Yes, it is true that autism can be lifelong condition but there are actually several treatments can help your child to acquire new skills and to prevail over a huge variety of developmental struggles. You should be aware that there are a lot of assistance that you can avail of to help meet the special needs of your autistic child. These programs include free services from the government, in-home behavioral therapies and programs that are based in schools. When you are able to build an effective treatment plan coupled with lots of love, guidance and support, your child can definitely learn, develop and flourish.

Do not wait for a diagnosis. When your child has autism, it means that he or she is delayed in several developmental areas. Therefore, the best thing that you can do to help your child is to begin treatment immediately. Look for help the instant you suspect that something is wrong with your child. Do not wait to see if your child will ultimately catch up with his or her peers or if he or she can eventually outgrow the problems that you notice. You do not even have to wait for an formal diagnosis. The sooner you child with autism gets help, the higher his or her chance of being treated successfully. The best way for you to expedite the development of your child and to lessen the symptoms and indications of autism is to have an early intervention.

Here are some valuable tips you can use if you have a child with autism:

- Learn more about the disorder. The more information and facts about autism that you, the better prepared you will be to make learned decisions for your child. You need to be educated about the different treatment alternatives available for your child. You need to ask the questions you have in mind and actively involve yourself in all the decisions being made about your child's treatments.

- Be an expert when it comes to your own child. You need to discover what specific things can trigger the "bad" or disrupting behaviors of your child as well as the specific things that can elicit positive responses from him or her. Which activities does your child find as very stressful or soothing or unpleasant or pleasurable? If you have a good understanding of which things, event and activities affect your child, you will be able to better troubleshoot problems and prevent the situations that result to your child's struggles and difficulties.

- Completely accept your child – peculiarities and all. Instead of focusing on how your child is not the same as the other "normal" children and what he or she is "missing out on", you can live with acceptance in your heart. Learn how to enjoy the peculiarities and quirks of your child. Celebrate his or her successes, no matter how small they may seem. And most importantly, stop measuring him up against other children. When your child feels that you love and accept him or her unconditionally, he will be more encouraged to do the things required for him to live a better life.

- Do not ever give up. It is really not possible to foresee how your child's autism will ultimately turn out. Do not readily jump into conclusions about how your child's life will be like. Like the rest of us, your child who has autism has the rest of his life to grow and develop into the best he can be.

Chapter 5: Autism Treatment

In the previous chapter, you've learned about guidelines in helping your child. It includes how to plan your child's treatments. In this chapter, we'll look into actual treatment options. You'll learn about recommended treatments and those that you better avoid.

Since the time autism was first recognized, people have formulated many approaches in treatment. Practice and success rates also evolved over the years. Some therapeutic programs focus on developing skills while attempting to replace the dysfunctional behaviors with more appropriate ones. Others focus on forming a learning environment to stimulate the child, designed to meet his special needs.

Through numerous studies, the factors that make certain approaches effective, whether in reversing or reducing the limitations caused by autism, were identified. Here are some factors that effective treatments share:

- They take into account the interests of the child.
- They have a predictable routine or schedule.
- They have tasks learned through simple steps/instructions.
- They have specially designed activities that effectively engage the child's attention.
- They use consistent reinforcement of behavior as basis.

- They involve a high amount of participation from the parents/guardian.

More and more programs today focus on the last item in the above list. Experts structure these programs in a manner that parents can ensure the therapy to continue at home. Well, you as the parent will be the one who spends the most time with the child. You are also the one who cares most for the child. Moreover, you are the child's earliest teacher. Results of studies show that parents/guardians who are trained well in working with the child in autism treatment can equal the effectiveness of professionals in the field.

Developmental Approach

There are different approaches in autism treatment. One of them is the developmental approach. Treatment programs that belong to this category provide the right amount of stimulation and provide structure and consistency for the child. They generally follow a determined schedule – giving the child an organized and planned experience. Such schedules are highly detailed. Not only do they indicate the time and activity, but the venue for each activity as well. For example, for a program done in a classroom, the facilitator would assign a particular area for each activity. With that setup, the children would know exactly what to expect. The developmental approach involves activities that encourage children to participate with their fellow students. The foremost principle is learning by doing.

Behaviorist Approach

The next is behaviorist approach. This approach operates on the positive reinforcement principle – people will more likely repeat or continue a behavior if they get a reward for it. In the behaviorist approach, a participating child will gain rewards upon performing or attempting to learn a new skill. This process is highly structured with carefully planned routines or cycles. If successful, the children will later perform the actions even without being told. The given rewards are aligned to what the child wants. They may be material or non-material things. Treatment programs under this approach are done up to 40 hours every week. They have shown the potential to teach children with autism near-normal behavior – at least those behaviors included in the program.

Be Wary: Nonstandard Approaches

Parents, together with other concerned individuals, are willing to do anything within their power to offer help to children with autism. Thus, numerous treatments have been formulated and parents are willing to try them upon learning about their existence. Some of these were developed by professionals, but some of them were not. These "non-professional" treatments don't show scientific evidence of success in treating children. There is some anecdotal support though. Without credible results from scientific studies, it's no wonder professionals don't recommend these treatments. Below are some of those treatments, also called nonstandard approaches:

• Facilitated communication is a treatment used particularly for autism patients who have trouble with verbal communication. The supporting person or facilitator guides the child's hands and fingers in operating a keyboard, typing his/her thoughts. The problem is that clinical study results show that the messages typed reflect more of the thoughts of the facilitator, not the child.

•   Holding therapy is an approach involving physical contact, particularly hugs. The parent would hug the child for long amounts of time frequently, even if the child resists. Those in support of the approach claim that such practice forms a substantial parent-child bond. Some of them also claim that it helps because it stimulates certain areas of the child's brain when it senses the boundaries of his/her own body. However, these claims aren't supported by scientific evidence.

•   Auditory integration training is an approach wherein the child is trained by requiring him/her to listen to a varied selection of sounds. The objective is to facilitate the development of the child's language comprehension. Those in support of the treatment claim that this helps by providing the child with balanced environmental stimuli. Scientific studies, though, found that this approach has about the same effectiveness as merely listening to music.

•   Dolman or Delcato method is an approach where the subjects are instructed to move the way they did during their early stages of development. The claim is that the participant learns the missing skills they should have developed at that stage. Again, this has no scientific evidence regarding its effectiveness.

The nonstandard approaches, as of now, are not proven to be effective by scientific studies. They may or may not help your child. Well, neither are they shown to be directly harmful. However, it is better to avoid them. Every bit of time allotted to your child's treatment is valuable. If it is spent on treatments that don't work, it won't help your child.

Chapter 6: Autism Management

Aside from the treatments discussed in the previous chapter, autism is handled by families through management – they opt for therapies. These are separated from treatments because they are not really designed to treat the condition – just manage it.

Autism therapies have two main goals:

• Reduce the abnormal behaviors and deficits connected to autism and other conditions within the ASD group.

• Improve the quality of life, as well as functional independence, of individuals with autism, particularly children.

Each therapy would have different specific objectives, but they'd fall into those two goals.

Therapies are divided into two major categories:

• Educational Intervention

• Medical Management

Aside from the specific activities done in these therapies with autistic individuals, they also usually involve support and training for the family members of the patient.

Many of the therapies might have similar activities and characteristics with treatments. However, therapies are separated from treatments for study purposes.

Educational Interventions

Let's first talk about educational interventions. These involve specialized curriculum for teaching autistic children academic subjects, along with traditional readiness skills, as they will find difficulty doing so in conventional schools. In addition, they also include education targeted towards improving spontaneity and functional communication, enhancing social skills, reduction of disruptive behavior, acquiring cognitive skills, and generalizing the skills they learned so they can apply them in separate situations. There are numerous models used – perhaps no two schools share exactly the same program. However, they frequently overlap and share several features including:

• Prompt intervention without waiting for a conclusive diagnosis;

• Extreme intervention – 25 hours per week at least and continues the whole year;

• Low ratio of student/teacher;

• Close involvement of family, particularly the training of parents;

• Interaction with NT or neurotypical (short for neurologically typical, a term used in the autism community referring to those who don't have ASD and/or other similar conditions) peers;

• Visually based training, like ABA and social stories;

• Structured to have predictable routines and definite physical boundaries – meant to minimize distraction; and

• Constant evaluation of a systematized intervention plan, which would be adjusted according to the results.

There are several intervention methods. Some are done in school, at home, or at a special center for autism. The facilitator may be the parents themselves, a teacher, speech therapist, and occupational therapist. In a study conducted in 2007, it was found that when a program based on a center is supplemented by a special education teacher's weekly home visits, it results to improvement of behavior and cognitive development.

Below are different intervention methods.

ABA

Applied Behavior Analysis (or ABA) is a field of applied research on behavior analysis science. Under this is an array of techniques for treating autism and several other diagnoses and behavior, counting rehab patients and those who need behavior change. Interventions based on ABA focus on learning tasks via one-on-one teaching that employs behaviorist principles – rooted on stimulus, response, and reward. They also focus on objective evaluation and dependable measurement of observable behavior. The professional behavioral analysis practice has substantial variation. The same is true among the interventions and assessments employed in school-based programs under ABA methods. ABA actually evolved from behavior modification. The latter only utilized reinforcement and punishment to accomplish behavior changed. ABA developed, adding replacement behavior strategies, functional analysis, data collection, and stimulus control.

The following are methods heavily based on ABA:

•   Early Intensive Behavioral Intervention. Like the name suggests, this method uses techniques early in the development of a child with autism intensively. The child will be taught foundational skills (e.g. attention, imitation, and compliance) using techniques of stimulus-response-reward nature. In addition, they also learn through naturalistic methods of teaching so they can generalize these skills.

A common technique is functional assessment. The teacher, in this case, creates a definitive description of a problem behavior. He/she will then identify the antecedents, consequences, and any other environmental factors that influence and maintain the behavior. He/she will form a hypothesis about the triggers of the behavior and collects data through observation to support the hypothesis. Controlled studies of ABA show improvements in several aspects (e.g. academic performance, language, and adaptive behavior) that are substantially better in comparison to the control groups.

•   Pivotal Response Therapy. This is a naturalistic method of intervention deriving principles from ABA. The difference is that it focuses on pivotal areas of the development of a child (e.g. motivation, social initiations, self-management, and responsiveness to multiple cues). The aim is to improve areas that have not been targeted specifically yet. It will be the participating child who decides the activities and objects to be used in the therapy. The facilitator uses "natural" reinforcement as rewards. The reinforcement is natural in the sense that it is the request of the child, not something arbitrarily decided by the facilitator.

• Aversive Therapy. In this therapy, the patients receive an electric shock to the skin with the aim to control behavior. This has been really controversial and not popular. It is only used in the Judge Rotenberg Educational Center.

Communication Intervention

Next type of educational intervention is Communication Intervention. In autism, the ability to communicate, whether verbally or non-verbally, is a main deficit. Children who have autism frequently engage into repetitive behavior because that is the only way they know how to convey their thoughts/feelings. This is why aiding a child in learning how to communicate his/her thoughts or needs is central to any intervention. Communication may be non-verbal or verbal depending on which is more effective for the child. To learn how to communicate intents, a child with autism needs extreme levels of intervention.

Like ABA, there are also different methods under Communication Intervention.

• SCERTS. This is a model used for instruction of children with ASD. It was structured with the objective of helping families, therapists, and educators cooperate with each other towards maximizing progress in aiding the child. It is actually an acronym representing three areas of focus. The first one is SC for social communication, which involves developing emotional expression and functional communication. The second one is ER for emotional regulation, which involves developing the ability to cope with stress and well-regulated emotions. The last one is TS for transactional support, which involves the use of support so families, therapists, and educators can effectively respond to the needs of the child, adapt the environment, and come up with tools to facilitate learning.

• Computer-assisted Therapy focused on Reasoning about Actions of Communication. Individuals who have autism experience difficulties in learning social rules via examples. Computer-assisted therapies for autism have been proposed to teach the rule directly along with examples. Long- and short-term evaluations have been done for a reasoning rehabilitation strategy. This method employs a mental simulator that is computer based with the ability to model emotional and mental states in the real world.

The reasoning performed by the simulator uses the belief-desire-intention model. At the start, the student learns basic concepts of knowledge and intention, eventually moving to more complex actions in communication like agreeing, explaining, and pretending.

Developmental

Next is Developmental models based on relationship. This approach gives importance to the relationships that aid children into reaching and mastering early milestones in development. These milestones (e.g. intentionality of action, intimacy with a caregiver, and interest in the world) are usually missed in autistic patients.

Here are the different methods within this type:

•   Relationship Development Intervention. This is a program for ASD patients based on the family. The rationale of this method is that developing dynamic intelligence (thinking flexibly, taking different perspectives, coping with change, and simultaneous processing of information) is crucial to the improvement of life quality of the patient.

•   Floortime or DIR. DIR stands for "Developmental, Individual Differences-based, Relationship-based." This is an approach of developmental intervention founded on the idea that autism's core deficits are individual differences within the sensory system, problems in motor planning, communication difficulties, relationship forming issues, and the individual's inability to connect his/her desire to communication and intentional action. Floortime's primary goal is to improve the language, cognitive, and social abilities of the child. As of now, these claims lack independent scientific research that supports the effectiveness of the method. So, treat it with some skepticism.

•   PLAY Project. This is an acronym that stands for Play and Language for Autistic Youngsters. This is a community-based program for autism training and early intervention which adopts concepts from DIR. In this approach, parents and professionals are trained to implement intensive developmental for young autistic children (from 18 months to 6 years). This program has been used since 2001 in around 100 agencies worldwide – 25 US states and 5 other countries.

•   Son-Rise. This is a home-based program. It involves the implementation of a sensory- and color-free playroom. The parents are trained first by an institute to accept their child fully without judgment before the implementation of the actual program. This is carried out through dialog sessions. In Son-Rise, the parents join with their child in his/her ritualistic behavior in order to strengthen the relationship – something similar with Floortime. The facilitator would continue to join them only through parallel play. The objective is to make the child more willing to engage.

TEACCH

Next we have Treatment and Education of Autistic and Related Communication Handicapped Children (TEACCH). Also referred to as "structured teaching," this approach follows highly structured schedules involving several tasks that the child performs guided by systematized visually structured activities, visual schedules, and organized physical environments. Parents are trained so that they can continue the program at home. There was a controlled study in 1998 that showed significantly more improvement in children who received TEACCH compared to the control group.

Recently, however, a meta-analysis in 2013 that compiled all the clinical trials of TEACCH showed that it actually had little to no improvements in several aspects including daily living activities, motor, cognitive, verbal, motor, and perceptual functioning, and communication skills. Positive effects, however, were found on social and disruptive behavior; though experts think this should still be looked more into because of methodological limitations.

Sensory Integration

Sensory Integration is another intervention. Atypical response to sensory stimuli is more prominent and common in autistic children. However, there is no solid evidence confirming sensory symptoms to separate the condition from other developmental disorders. There are several approaches that focus on sensory aspects. However, all of them lack support from empirical evidence.

Animal-assisted Therapy

Next is Animal-assisted Therapy. As the name suggests, this approach makes use of a companion animal (such as a dog) as an integral part of the therapy. This therapy remains controversial as of today, but there was a meta-analysis that shows moderate improvement in patient's autism symptoms. One kind of this approach is dolphin-assisted therapy. There were studies that support it, but reviews have found flaws in the methodology. It's still not yet clear whether the therapy is actually effective or if it just gives patients an improved mood.

Neurofeedback

Then, we have Neurofeedback. This kind of therapy is done by allowing an autistic individual to directly observe his or her brain activity. The objective is to give the patient the ability to regulate his or her own brainwave patterns. The most conventional form of this is a computer audiovisual display akin to a game that gets feed from EEG electrode output. In evaluations, positive results have been found for ASD; though it is pointed out that studies don't have enough randomness in assignment of controls.

Another therapeutic approach is Patterning. This is an exercise set that has an objective of improving the organization of the neurologic impairments of a child. Patterning has been in use for decades for the management of autism and other neurologic disorders. Experts note that the theories used as basis for the method are oversimplified. Moreover, it is not supported by thoroughly designed studies.

Packing

Packing is a therapy reserved for autistic children who are prone to harming themselves, most of them unable to speak. It is done by tightly wrapping the child up in refrigerated wet sheets except for the head. Frequency can be up to several times a week, and may be continued for years. Similar techniques have been from centuries ago to control violent patients, but the modern use started in France starting from 1960s. Today, packing is widely used in French clinics. While the same principles have been used for a long time, there is no scientific evidence yet of its effectiveness for autism. Concern is even raised regarding probable adverse effects on health.

Transcranial Magnetic Stimulation

Next we have Transcranial Magnetic Stimulation. This therapy is actually a recognized, to some extent, treatment for depression. It has been proposed for autism and other ASDs. However, a review was published in 2013 that declares insufficient evidence that it helps with ASD.

Medical Management

You've seen the therapies under educational intervention. Now, let's move to medical management. This involves therapies that use diets, drugs, and supplements for relieving common symptoms of autism that can be influenced by physiology (e.g. seizures, hyperactivity, irritability, and sleeping difficulties). The belief is that physiology can be altered through those means to accomplish the said objective.

Anecdotal evidence is abundant in support of medical management. Many parents who tried at least one therapy reported progress. There are some well-publicized reports of children who managed to return to conventional education after therapy. These reports are accompanied by accounts of substantial health and well-being improvement. However, it's probable that these reports are cases of autistic children who haven't received treatment growing up. The reports are also hard to verify and they almost never mention negative outcomes. In terms of medical therapies that have scientific support, there are only a few.

Below are some medical management techniques in practice today.

Drugs

There are several medications that are being used for managing problems branching from ASD. Above 50% of diagnosed children in the US receive a prescription of anticonvulsants or psychoactive drugs; the most common of these are antipsychotics, stimulants, and antidepressants. Antipsychotics are the only ones that showed efficacy.

Research on medicines for autism focused mostly on atypical antipsychotics, particularly risperidone – the one with the greatest amount of evidence showing improvements with autism-associated tantrums, aggression, irritability, and self-injury. This drug is approved by the FDA for treatment of irritability arising as a symptom of autism. Short-term trials (at most six months) show only mild to moderate adverse effects. At most, only monitoring is needed in terms of high blood sugar, drowsiness and weight gain. Long-term safety and efficacy is not yet fully determined. It is also not clear whether risperidone helps with communication and social deficits. The FDA's approval has specifications though: it is not recommended for children who only have mild or occasional aggression.

There are other drugs prescribed, but off-label. What this means is that they are not approved for ASD treatment.

Supplements

Vitamin and mineral supplements are used because it is believed that deficiencies in nutrients trigger autism. The most common practice among parents is giving their children supplements of B vitamin as the vitamin creates enzymes that the brain needs. Another is magnesium. While this practice helps in overall health, there is no scientific proof yet of effectiveness in autism. At most, they are only shown to relieve symptoms.

Diets

Special diets have been formulated for children with autism. Research suggests that autistic children suffer difficulties in digesting proteins, especially gluten and casein. Seeds of oat, wheat, barley plants, and rye contain gluten. Dairy products contain casein. Many autistic children are fed with gluten-free and/or casein-free diets.

There are a few more elimination diets formulated for children with autism. Some target food dyes, salicylates, simple sugars, and yeast. There is no scientific evidence yet supporting these special diets. Moreover, elimination diets require precise monitoring to ensure they don't create deficiencies in nutrition – which will only cause harm to the child.

Hormonal

A hormone called Secretin has been studied and found to improve social and communication skills in autistic children. However, a research has found that it has the same level of improvements as placebo.

Chelation Therapy

There is speculation regarding heavy metal poisoning that it triggers autism symptoms. Thus, there are some parents who turned to detoxification methods via chelation therapy. However, evidence supporting the effectiveness of this practice is anecdotal at best. After all, its basis is pure speculation as of now.

Chiropractic

An alternative medical practice called Chiropractic has been proposed for autism management. The hypothesis is that disorders in the spine of mechanical nature negatively affect general health through the nervous system. Thus, treatment can be done with spinal manipulation. Many professionals in this method reject vaccination since vaccines are equal to poison in traditional chiropractic philosophy. Some even claim that vaccines themselves cause autism. Chiropractic treatment, however, doesn't have enough supporting evidence that it can help in medical conditions save back pain. Moreover, there is no conclusive evidence regarding chiropractic care for autism.

Craniosacral Therapy

Another alternative medical practice proposed for autism is craniosacral therapy. This one revolves around the hypothesis that rhythmic impulses sent through cerebrospinal fluid are affected by cranial suture restrictions. It is believed that by applying gentle pressure on the external skull areas can improve the balance and flow of the fluid to the brain and result in relief of symptoms of many conditions. The underlying theory lacks scientific support, same as the therapy.

Electroconvulsive Therapy

According to studies, 12-17% of autism patients in the adolescent to young adult age group are positive of catatonia – hyperactive motor activity loss. Electroconvulsive therapy (or ECT) has been used for treating cases of catatonia as well as related conditions associated with autism. However, no studies have ever been done for ECT's effectiveness in actually treating autism. Moreover, there are legal and ethical obstacles to its practice.

Hyperbaric Oxygen Therapy

There was a study in 2009 that presented show immediate and significant improvement on the behavior of autistic children after 40 hourly therapies of 24% oxygen with a pressure of 1.3 atmospheres. This is not yet independently confirmed. The method is called hyperbaric oxygen therapy. This is one of the more expensive therapy options. With uncertain conclusions, this makes it a risky option.

Stem cell therapy

Stem cell therapy has also been proposed for autism management. However, the proposal has not yet been tested. The potential is still there, but for now, it is only a probable future treatment.

Other Types

There are many more types of management techniques aside from medical and educational interventions.

Environmental Enrichment

Therapies under environmental enrichment are rooted from the concept that the brain is affected by the information processing coming from the surroundings. With the right stimulation, the brain can develop better.

• Massage therapy. This was reviewed on its potential for symptomatic treatment for autism. Evidence is limited at best.

- Music therapy. This approach uses music to allow patients to communicate their feelings. There were improvements found, albeit short-term, in gestural and verbal communication, but no effects on concerns regarding behavior.

Parent-mediated interventions

Parent-mediated interventions are also practiced. These are interventions offering counseling and support to parents who have autistic children. The benefits are not directly towards children with autism, but rather on the parents. They have been found to be effective in reducing maternal depression and other stresses to the parents.

Other Alternative Practices

A number of alternative medicines have been proposed. This includes acupuncture. No alternative medicine has been proven effective yet.

Religious

In some cases, interventions of a religious nature were used to deal with autism. They have not been scientifically proven. They'll never be perhaps because of the nature of these methods. Believers find no reason to test them after all.

Too Much Uncertainty?

As you probably have noticed, most therapies lack sufficient scientific evidence to be reliable, especially those that are outside the two main categories. It is no wonder why there are so many treatments and therapies out there for autism, but only a few that has significant findings of effectiveness. The condition, despite having a long history behind it, is still not fully understood whether it comes to its causes or mechanisms. You might think that this doesn't bode well for the hopes of your child with autism. There is another perspective to consider here. With so many unproven treatments and therapies, you can narrow down your options quite easily. It can allow you to easily choose treatment or management methods and act early which is important. You'll learn more about choosing treatments in a later chapter.

Chapter 7: Autism Awareness

Autism awareness, like in many neurological disorders, had gone through many changes as time passed by. Even today, autism is not yet fully understood. It is not impossible to find people who are prejudiced against people with autism. It's not that much of a problem if they just ignore autistic people, but there are some who would make fun of the disorder and the afflicted.

In the early days, primitive knowledge resulted to people with autism or other disorders to be looked down on by people. Extremely religious ones will even say that it is a "punishment by higher power" or a "curse due to the sin of parents." Others think the afflicted are possessed by demons. There are still some who have this line of thinking today bringing forth the religious intervention methods described in the previous chapter.

Later on, knowledge fortunately became advanced. The fields of medicine and psychology have made new discoveries and milestones. Unfortunately, this didn't automatically make it better for autism. Between the 1950s and the 1980s, the dominant theory regarding autism is that it was caused by bad parenting. Particularly, the "refrigerated mother theory" was widely accepted. The theory states that a mother who is emotionally cold results into a child who is autistic. This was proposed by Bruno Bettelheim, a child psychologist. Now we know that is incorrect. Autism doesn't stem from the way the child was raised. It is inborn wherein the child inherited a susceptibility to the condition.

With the limited understanding of the condition, many more misconceptions, such as the refrigerated mother theory mentioned above, and myths surrounding autism exist. Some of them carry negativity mostly stated by people who don't know anything about the condition or has never lived with or closely known somebody who has it. Some may ring positive at first but they can actually be harmful if not corrected. Well, these are mostly stated by people who have good intentions towards people with autism but like in the previous case, they don't have substantial knowledge of autism. All they know about autism is probably from TV shows, movies, and other fictional works which aren't really credible sources especially for sensitive topics like this.

In a previous chapter, you have learned that getting to know more about autism will have benefits for you and your child. Taking note of these misconceptions will be a good start. Knowing the truth behind them will allow you to correctly dismiss negative opinions about your child, answer the questions of those with sincere concern, and keep your own thoughts positive so you have accurate expectations about your child. Here are some of those misconceptions:

• Autism is relatively new. The truth: It was first described in 1943 by Leo Kranner, a scientist. However, the earliest description of a child who is now confirmed to have had the condition was found in a written account from 1799.

• People who didn't meet the criteria of autism diagnosis will never show characteristics similar to those who met it. The truth: They can. The characteristics of autism exist in a continuum that encompasses those considered "normal." They may be shown by non-autistic people to a lesser extent.

• Autism is a mental health disorder. The truth: It is a neurological disorder characterized by abnormalities in neurotransmitter levels and brain structure. The classifications are related yet different.

• Vaccines cause autism. The truth: No evidence has been found to prove this. There was indeed a study, back in 1998, that linked autism with childhood vaccination but it was retracted long ago because the results lack credibility.

• The cause of autism is exclusively environmental factors. The truth: Like discussed in the first chapter, autism has several probable causes. There is actually strong evidence that genetics is more likely than environmental factors.

• Autistic individuals are violent. The truth: This is a common misconception for many neurological disorders. If we look at statistics, those who don't have such disorders are actually more likely to hurt other people. Only a small percentage of autistic individuals are prone to violent outbursts and even then, they rarely cause harm to other people.

• Autistic individuals can't or doesn't want to have meaningful social relationships. The truth: They have difficulties with communication and social interaction but they are not devoid of ability to form relationships. Many autistic people have successfully had families.

•   Every autistic individual has savant abilities. The truth: The prevalence of savant abilities is higher in people with autism than "normal" people. Kim Peek is an autistic person who read over 7,000 books and can recall 80% of the content with photographic accuracy. He can also pinpoint the day of the week a person was born just by knowing the birth date. Daniel Tammet is another autistic person. He can recite pi up to 20,000 digits and speaks 10 languages fluently. He was even able to invent his own language. However, only 10% of autistic individuals exhibit such savant abilities.

•   Autistic individuals don't have empathic feelings. The truth: They are capable of feelings and in many cases actually turn out to be more empathic than the average "normal" human. They only express it in ways that are more difficult to recognize.

•   Autistic individuals are mentally retarded. The truth: People with autism and other conditions under ASD are unique. Only a few have been found to have mental disabilities. Some may appear to be unintelligent but possess higher level of understanding than the average person. Some may show difficulties in simple tasks but accomplish and master more complex tasks easily. Many autistic individuals have been able to earn a college degree and succeed in life. Dr. Temple Grandin is a famous person who overcame autism and went on to be highly successful – becoming a professor of Animal Science (Colorado State University), authored four books (one of which is a New York Times bestseller), and designed worldwide-used facilities for handling livestock.

• Autism can be cured. The truth: Well, maybe. Someday. But right now, there is no known cure for it.

• Treatments work across the board. The truth: Autism-associated symptoms and behaviors are far too many and each patient may exhibit a unique set from another. As you will learn in the last chapter of this book, treatment plans work best if they are customized according to the individual's needs.

Autism Advocacies

There are existing movements dedicated to autism and they have varying perspectives. There are those who think autism should not be labeled as a disorder. Instead, it should be seen as variation in functioning. They believe that the society is unnecessarily burdened in caring for autistic individuals.

Some think that autistic people have a culture of their own. They compare it to being born among people speaking a different language or have a different philosophy or religion.

Advocates of autism believe that the genes for autism should not be removed. This is rooted still in the belief that autism is a natural human variation rather than a disorder. On a related note, they think finding a cure for autism is offensive. Instead of searching for a cure, they advocate acceptance.

However these perspectives go, it won't matter which ones you choose to believe. The important thing is to support your child and always think what is best for him/her.

Chapter 8: How You Can Help Your Child

Provide structure and safety.

Being armed with enough knowledge and information about autism and being completely involved in the treatment of your child's autism can really go a long way towards assisting your child. In addition, the tips below can also help in making the day to day living in your home a lot easier not only for your autistic child but for you and the whole family, as well.

- Be consistent. Your child with autism may find it difficult to adapt the things he or she has learned in one setting like in the office of the therapist or at school to another place including your home. For instance, your child may have learned how to use sign language at school in order to communicate with his teachers and classmates but he may not think that he needs to do the same at home. When you are able to create consistency in the different environments of your child, you will be able to greatly reinforce all the learning's that he or she has acquired. Therefore, you will need to ask the therapists and teachers of your child about what they do during therapy or classroom sessions so you can apply the same techniques in your own home. It is also advisable that you explore the possibility of your child taking his therapy sessions in different locations so that he will be more encouraged to carry out the lessons he has learned in different environments. It is also vital that you become consistent in how you interact with your child and how you deal with his or her difficult behaviors.

- Stick to a schedule. It has been noted that children with autism have the tendency to perform at their best when they follow a highly structured schedule or routine. This is because they do not only need consistency in their lives but they actually crave for it. Therefore, it is highly recommended that you create a schedule that your child can follow that includes consistent times for their meals, therapy sessions, school classes and bedtime. As much as possible, avoid disrupting your child's routine. If you can foresee that an unavoidable alteration in his routine will occur, make sure that you prepare your child ahead of time.

- Reward your child for good behavior. When you give your child positive reinforcements, they will be greatly motivated to continue doing the positive things that they are being taught to do. Do not be stop yourself from praising your child when you see him or her acting properly or when he or she has learned a new skill. But make sure that you specifically tell them which particular behavior you are rewarding him or her for. Try different ways of rewarding your child for behaving properly. You can choose to give him or her stickers or allowing your child to play with his or her favorite toys.

- Establish a safety zone in your home. Create a private area in your home where your child can freely relax while feeling secure and being safe. This means that you have to organize and set boundaries in your home in such a manner that your child can comprehend. It is ideal if you can use visual cues like colored tape to mark the areas in your house that are off limits to your child and picture labels on the items in your house. Make sure that you safety proof that whole house, especially the areas where your child frequently goes to avoid injuries when your child goes into his tantrums or other behaviors that are self-injurious.

Look for non-verbal ways to connect to your child.

It is really challenging to make a connection with your child who has autism. But you do not really need to speak or talk in order for you to converse and bond with your child. You can communicate with your child by the way you look at him or her or the way you touch him or her and the tone of voice and body language that you use . You also need to realize that your child is actually communicating with you even if you do not him or her speak. You just need to make the effort of learning the language that your child uses.

- Look for non-verbal cues. You need to be observant and mindful of your child's actions so you will be able to become familiar with the non-verbal cues that your child uses to communicate. You need to pay close attention to the specific kinds of sounds that your child makes, his or her facial expressions and gestures. What does he say when he is happy? What sounds does he make when he is feeling tired? What gestures does he use when he wants something?

- Figure out your child's needs behind his or her tantrums. All of us can feel upset and disturbed when we are misunderstood or disregarded. And it is the same for your child who has autism. When your child acts out, it usually means that you are not able to pick up the non-verbal cues that your child is giving you. Remember that your child will normally throw a tantrum when he or she wants to communicate his frustration and get your attention.

- Make enough time for fund. Always keep in mind that your autistic child is just like any other kid. You and your child need to have more to life than therapy sessions. Make sure that you include playtime in your child's schedule when he or she is most alert. Discover ways on how you can spend fun times with your child by considering the things that can make your child smile, laugh and be more socially interactive. Your child will most likely to take pleasure in the activities that you have set out for him or her when they do not appear to be therapeutic or instructive. There are a number of great benefits that can result from your delight in keeping your child company and from your child's delight in spending free and fun times with you. Make sure that you treat play as a vital part in your child's learning and you should not look at it as work or something tedious.

- Pay close attention to the sensory sensitivities of your child. A lot of children coping with autism have hypersensitivity to various lights, sounds, touches, tastes and smells. But there are also children with autism who have under-sensitivity to sensory stimuli.

You need to determine what particular sight, sound, smell, movement and tactile sensation that trigger the "bad" or disrupting behaviors of your child and which particular ones elicit positive responses.

Create a customized autism treatment plan for your child.

With all the various treatments available to help your child with autism, it can be very difficult to work out which particular approach is appropriate for your child. It can even seem more confusing and complicated when you hear different people and doctors give varying or even contradictory recommendations for your child. When you are trying to put together a treatment plan for your child's autism, it is important that you do not think that any one particular treatment plan will work the same way for everyone. Each person who has autism has his own uniqueness with varying strengths and weaknesses.

The treatment plan for your child should be customized based on his or her unique needs. You should be the person who knows your child best and because of that, you should have the capacity to know whether a particular plan meets your child's needs or not. You can do this by posing these questions to yourself:

- What strengths does my child have?

- Which of my child's behaviors cause the most issues and problems?

- What particular essential skills does my child lack?

- What particular learning style does my child have – seeing, listening or doing?

- Which particular activities does my child enjoy the most and how can these activities be incorporated in his treatment plan?

Lastly, you need to remember that no matter which specific treatment plan you choose for your child, your participation is the key to success. You will enable your child to take full advantage of the treatment plan if you are able to work hand in hand with the team or group that handles your child's treatment and you are able to follow through with therapy in your own home.

How to choose treatments for your child's autism

The different treatments that were created to help people with autism were designed with different objectives in mind. Some treatment plans can help in lessening the difficult behaviors of your child, or in helping your child to be able to communicate and socialize better or in dealing with the problems your child have with regards to sensory integration, motor skill, emotional concerns and sensitivities to food.

Because you will be faced with a lot of choices, it is very essential that you take your time in doing research by talking to different treatment experts and asking all the questions you might have in mind. But always remember that you do not really have to select just one kind of treatment therapy. Your objective should be to create a treatment plan that will deal with all of the symptoms and needs of your child. Sometimes, you will only able to do this by combining different treatment approaches so you can take advantage of the strengths of each treatment approach. The most common treatment approaches that you will find out include behavioral therapy, speech language therapy, play based therapy, physical and occupational therapy and nutritional therapy.

Find help and support for your child.

You must already be aware of the fact that caring for your child who has autism can be very demanding and can take up a lot of your time and energy. It is expected that there will really be days when you may feel overwhelmed, weighed down, stressed out or altogether discouraged. Parenting itself is not easy. But it can become more difficult and challenging when you are raising an autistic child. You will not be the best parent for your child if you are not able to take proper care of yourself. Just like what they say during plane rides, put on your gas mask first before you attempt to help your child on his or her gas mask. You will not be able to help your child if you yourself feels weak and discouraged. Do not attempt to do all things on your own. You need to realize that you do not really have to. There are a lot of places that families like yours who have autistic children can rely on for advice, support and encouragement.

- There are several autism support groups you can join. These groups are actually a good way for you to meet and interact with other families who are going through the same problems and challenges that your family is facing. The parents in these groups willingly share information, experiences and pieces of advice with one another. You can also find people who are willing to offer their shoulders for you to lean on to get the emotional support that you need. A lot of parents with autistic children report that merely being around with other people who share their experience is a big help already. It is so easy for parents to isolate themselves when they receive their child's autism diagnosis. You can reduce this isolation by surrounding yourself with people who will not judge you and will willingly offer help to you.

- There is also respite care that you can turn to. All parents, even those who have "normal" children, need a break from time to time. But for parents like you who cope with the additional stress of autism, this fact is particularly true. When you avail of a respite care, there will be another caregiver who will take over your role as a parent on a temporary basis. This will give you the chance to take a break for a couple of hours or several days or even several weeks if you prefer to.

- You can also opt to go through an individual counseling, marital counseling or family counseling. You should not be embarrassed to admit when you are feeling stressed out, anxious or depressed. You need to always have an honest evaluation of yourself so you can get the help that you need. You may opt to go to a therapist on your own where you can have a secure place to voice out your thoughts and feelings – including those that are good, bad and ugly. Your therapist can help you sort out your thoughts and feelings and determine the best way to manage them. There are also times when autism can take its toll on your marriage or on your family as a whole. Going to a marriage counseling or a family therapy can aid in working out the problems and issues that you are facing.

Conclusion

Thank you again for purchasing this book!

I hope this book was able to help you to better understand how you can deal with your child's autism and the things that you can do to help your child live a better life.

The next step is to reflect and determine how you can apply the techniques and strategies that you have just learned in your own life.

Finally, if you enjoyed this book, please take the time to share your thoughts and post a review on Amazon. We do our best to reach out to readers and provide the best value we can. Your positive review will help us achieve that. It'd be greatly appreciated!

Thank you and good luck!

Check Out My Other Books

Below you'll find some of my other popular books that are popular on Amazon and Kindle as well. Simply click on the links below to check them out. Alternatively, you can visit my author page on Amazon to see other work done by me.

ADHD Symptoms & Strategies

http://amzn.to/P4nAtL

Cure For Controlling People

http://amzn.to/1jGkVBD

Narcissism Unleashed!

http://amzn.to/1jJrinG

Curing Workaholics

http://amzn.to/1pb5O8V

Mind Control Mastery

http://amzn.to/Rti71I

The Ultimate Self Esteem Guide

http://amzn.to/1tNW4Bm

The Shopping Addiction

http://amzn.to/QIhi4y

Living With OCD

http://amzn.to/1mp0rll

BOX SET #1 Narcissism Unleashed & Cure For Controlling People

http://amzn.to/1uUGK6o

BOX SET #2 Narcissism Unleashed & Mind Control Mastery

http://amzn.to/1ombagm

BOX SET #3 ADHD Symptoms & Strategies & Living With OCD

http://amzn.to/1uUERXq

BOX SET #4 Living With OCD & Ultimate Self Esteem Guide

http://amzn.to/1slhJNF

BOX SET #5 Living With OCD & Ultimate Self Esteem & Narcissism & Mind Control & Shopping Addiction

http://amzn.to/1ioc84q

BOX SET #6 Ultimate Self Esteem Guide & Narcissism Unleashed

http://amzn.to/ZoDFWN

BOX SET #7 Ultimate Self Esteem Guide & Mind Control Mastery

http://amzn.to/1CaxfDX

If the links do not work, for whatever reason, you can simply search for these titles on the Amazon website to find them.